D1604562

FAKE NEWS
and the Manipulation of Public Opinion

Carla Mooney

ReferencePoint
Press®

San Diego, CA

© 2019 ReferencePoint Press, Inc.
Printed in the United States

For more information, contact:
ReferencePoint Press, Inc.
PO Box 27779
San Diego, CA 92198
www.ReferencePointPress.com

LIBRARY OF CONGRESS CATALOGING-IN-PUBLICATION DATA

Names: Mooney, Carla, 1970– author.
Title: Fake News and the Manipulation of Public Opinion/by Carla Mooney.
Description: San Diego, CA: ReferencePoint Press, Inc., 2018. | Includes
    bibliographical references and index.
Identifiers: LCCN 2018041101 (print) | LCCN 2018047066 (ebook) | ISBN
    9781682825402 (eBook) | ISBN 9781682825396 (hardback)
Subjects: LCSH: Fake news—United States—Juvenile literature. | Mass media
    and public opinion—United States—Juvenile literature.
Classification: LCC PN4888.F35 (ebook) | LCC PN4888.F35 M66 2018 (print) |
    DDC 302.230973—dc23

LC record available at https://lccn.loc.gov/2018041101

CONTENTS

INTRODUCTION

Manipulating Public Opinion

The ability to manipulate public opinion online has reached unprecedented levels of sophistication. It has taken less than a decade to get to that point. At a 2010 conference, computer scientist Filippo Menczer listened to a speaker talk about fake news reports that had gone viral during a Massachusetts special Senate election. Menczer was deeply interested in the presentation, as he and his colleagues at Indiana University–Bloomington had been tracking what they called "social spam" on the Internet. "People were creating social sites with junk on them, and getting money from the ads,"[1] he says. Purposely creating entirely false content and actively spreading it online was not something Menczer had seen before. He firmly believed this was just the beginning. And he was right.

By 2014, Menczer and other social media researchers were noting a number of fake stories online. Some were political; others were cultural. Many aimed to arouse public fear. For example, false stories circulating online in 2014 stirred fears about immigrants arriving in the United States carrying the deadly Ebola virus. "Some politicians wanted to close the airports, and I think a lot of that was motivated by the efforts to sow panic,"[2] says Menczer. By the 2016 US presidential election, the stream of fake news online had become a raging torrent. During the months before and after the election, fake news headlines lured millions of social media users on Facebook, Twitter, and YouTube into clicking on and then spreading false reports that had the potential to manipulate public opinion on both issues and candidates.

Sophisticated Manipulation

Digital technologies—in particular the Internet and social media—have created ideal tools for manipulating public opinion. It takes some expertise, but a lot of people nowadays have that capability. It requires someone who knows how to gather personal data (such as an individual's opinions, tastes, and background) from social media sites and other online activity. With this information he or she can determine who is most likely to be influenced by a certain message—and then target those individuals with fabricated stories. The manipulation of public opinion sometimes goes beyond fake news. Hackers can—and do—infiltrate private e-mail servers and computer networks, steal sensitive information that has been stored or transmitted online, and release it at a time chosen to have the maximum impact on public opinion.

Fake news is often skillfully manipulated to look as if it comes from reputable news outlets. It spreads online because many people are willing to believe the false article and share it with others. During the weeks leading up to the 2016 presidential election, a story claiming that Pope Francis (the leader of the Roman Catholic Church) had endorsed Republican candidate Donald Trump began to circulate online. The story was originally published by a website calling itself WTOE 5 News. It quoted the pope as saying he had decided to endorse Trump after the FBI chose to not prosecute Democratic candidate Hillary Clinton for several alleged crimes. Although the website name resembled the names of reputable news agencies, it was anything but that. Anyone who bothered to look a little further might have come across the site's "about us" page, where it identified itself as a fantasy news website. The story was picked up by other sites. Its spread suggests that few people took the time to check out the source. According to an analysis by the Internet media company Buzzfeed News, the fake news story had nearly a million user engagements on Facebook by November 8—election day. Although the story was completely false, according to Buzzfeed, it became

Smartphones and social media are ideal tools for manipulating public opinion. Fake news headlines, stories, and images have lured millions of people into clicking on and spreading false information.

one of the most widely circulated fake news stories on Facebook before the election.

Although experts cannot say whether a single fake news story affected the election's outcome, they believe that stories like this one might have influenced the views of some voters toward the candidates. A 2018 study by researchers at Ohio State University suggests that about 4 percent of people who supported President Barack Obama (a Democrat) for reelection in 2012 were influenced to not vote for Hillary Clinton (also a Democrat) in 2016 because they believed fake news stories leading up to the election. "We cannot prove that belief in fake news *caused* these former Obama voters to defect from the Democratic candidate in 2016," wrote the researchers. "These data strongly suggest, however, that exposure to fake news did have a significant impact on voting decisions."[3]

A Growing Problem

As more fake news circulates online, the power of these false stories to create doubt and confusion among readers and manipulate public opinion is becoming a bigger problem. Technology experts like Or Levi believe the prevalence of fake news and the problems that it causes will only grow in the future. Levi is the founder of an Israeli start-up company called AdVerif.ai that develops ways to use artificial intelligence to fight fake news. "There are reports which are predicting that within three to four years, people in advanced economies will consume more false content than true content, which is really mind-blowing,"[4] says Levi.

As more fake content appears online, people are finding it increasingly difficult to determine which stories are true and which are fake. As a result, public trust in the media is plunging. According to a 2018 Monmouth University poll, 77 percent of Americans believe that traditional television and newspaper media outlets report fake news at least occasionally, with 31 percent saying it happens regularly. In addition, 83 percent of Americans believe that outside groups are actively trying to push fake news stories into the mainstream media, and 66 percent believe this is a serious problem. "These findings are troubling, no matter how you define 'fake news,'" says Patrick Murray, director of the Monmouth University Polling Institute. "Confidence in an independent fourth estate [news media] is a cornerstone of a healthy democracy. Ours appears to be headed for the intensive care unit."[5]

The problem extends beyond the United States. According to a 2018 report by the global communications and public relations firm Edelman, overall trust in traditional media is dropping globally. In a survey of more than thirty-three thousand people across

> "There are reports which are predicting that within three to four years, people in advanced economies will consume more false content than true content, which is really mind-blowing."[4]
>
> —Or Levi, the founder of the artificial intelligence company AdVerif.ai

twenty-eight countries, Edelman found that nearly two-thirds of respondents (66 percent) believe that media organizations are more concerned with drawing in a bigger audience than accurate reporting. Almost as many, 65 percent, believe that media organizations would sacrifice accuracy in reporting in order to be the first to report a story. And almost 60 percent believe that the media is more likely to support a political position than accurately inform the public. Slowing the tide of fake news will require cooperation on a mass scale. Governments, technology companies, news media, and the public will need to work together to develop ways to combat fake news and minimize the influence it has on public opinion. "What we want to convey most," says Menczer, "is that fake news is a real problem, it's a tough problem, and it's a problem that requires serious research to solve."[6]

"What we want to convey most is that fake news is a real problem, it's a tough problem, and it's a problem that requires serious research to solve."[6]

—Computer scientist Filippo Menczer

CHAPTER ONE

The New Look of Fake News

Although fake news has become one of the hottest topics of the twenty-first century, it is nothing new. In fact, it has existed for generations.

The Early Days of Fake News

In the early days of the United States, President John Adams lamented that a free press would not lead to a more informed public because "there has been more new error propagated by the press in the last ten years than in [the] hundred years before 1798."[7] When discussing Adams's writing at an American Historical Association panel about early America and fake news, historian Katlyn Carter noted that fake news was a problem as far back as colonial America. "A lot of things we talk about today we talk about as unprecedented," says Carter. "It's important to look back and see how these same concerns and issues have been raised at many points throughout history."[8]

During that same era, British loyalist Thomas Hutchinson, who served as the royal governor of the Massachusetts Bay Colony from 1771 through 1774, expressed his frustration at the false stories being written in the press. In particular, Hutchinson took exception to the reporting of Samuel Adams. Adams was a leader in the Sons of Liberty, a secret society formed to stand up for the rights of the American colonists. Adams's writing for the *Boston Gazette* newspaper was notorious for being light on facts. "It might well have been the best fiction written in the English language for the entire period,"[9] writes media historian Eric

Burns. Hutchinson worried that most New England residents were reading—and believing—articles filled with false information. In 1765 a group of arsonists burned Hutchinson's house to the ground. Because of false reporting in the *Gazette*, they wrongly believed he supported the Stamp Act, a tax on newspapers and other written documents imposed by the British Parliament on the American colonies. "They were old men, young men, and boys barely old enough to read, all of them jacked up on ninety-proof Sam Adams prose,"[10] writes Burns.

Spreading Ideas Faster and Farther

Although fake news has existed for centuries, technology is changing how it spreads. Throughout history, advances in technology have made it possible for ideas to spread more quickly. With the invention of the printing press in the fifteenth century, for example, knowledge and ideas could be shared faster and more cheaply and by more people than ever before. Centuries later the invention of radio and television brought news and ideas from around the world directly into people's homes.

In the digital age, advances like the Internet, social media, and mobile devices are spreading ideas faster and farther than at any other time in history. The connectivity of digital technologies has erased traditional barriers. Physical borders, time, and distance have been rendered nearly meaningless in the context of communication and information sharing. This same technology has also increased the reach of fake news and the speed at which it travels. A story concocted by one person on a laptop in the United States can be uploaded to a blog or shared across social media in countries around the world. Hundreds, thousands, or even millions of people can see and share that same story in a matter of minutes or even seconds.

Creating and distributing content is easy thanks to the Internet. People routinely share information through blogs, websites, videos, photographs, and social media. Some of it is legitimate. Some of it is fabricated. Either way, all it takes is a computer and an Internet connection.

Deaths in India

Fake news can have deadly consequences. In India, more than 200 million people use the messaging service WhatsApp to stay in touch with family and friends. Many users, however, are inexperienced with smartphones and are easily fooled by fake news that spreads quickly through the app. False stories accusing people of child trafficking, organ harvesting, or other heinous activities are rampant on the app and are causing chaos in some Indian villages.

In recent months, dozens of people have been lynched by mobs after false stories circulated. In one example, a tech worker and his friends were returning home to his native village when they encountered a mob that was convinced they were child kidnappers because of rumors spread on WhatsApp. Initially, the tech worker and his friends were able to drive away, but details identifying their van spread quickly. The mob stopped them again. This time, they killed one of the men in the van. To stop the violence, many communities are making efforts to disprove rumors before a mob forms. In some communities, local police are setting up a WhatsApp group so citizens can check in to verify whether information they encounter online is true.

Through social media sites, users can even target specific individuals or groups who are most likely to be receptive to the content. Lisa-Maria Neudert, a researcher with the Oxford Internet Institute, has studied how fake news stories and related content were shared on social media sites like Twitter and Facebook. "This ability to have mass distribution at extremely low cost enables propaganda at an entirely different scale, one we've never seen before," Neudert says. "And it uses all of the information that we as users are consciously and unconsciously providing, to produce individualized propaganda."[11]

What Is Fake News?

While the phrase *fake news* appears all over the media today, the definition of what it includes is not always clear. The simplest description is this: fake news is fabricated news or information

School shooting survivor Emma González (with mic) speaks at a 2018 protest march in Washington, DC. A video that was altered to make it look like she was tearing up the US Constitution circulated widely over the Internet.

that is meant to be perceived as factual. In 2017, for example, several fake news websites reported that US House minority leader Nancy Pelosi's daughters were arrested for trafficking cocaine. In fact, Pelosi's daughters had not been arrested for smuggling drugs or anything else. Fake news can also take the form of manipulated videos or photographs meant to create or support a false narrative. In 2018, for instance, a video of Emma González, a survivor of the mass shooting at Marjory Stoneman Douglas High School in Parkland, Florida, was altered to show her ripping up the US Constitution. In fact, she was tearing up a gun-target poster in a picture for a *Teen Vogue* article about gun control. The altered image was intended to communicate the idea that González supported taking away rights granted in the Constitution.

The fake news label is often misused. Errors in news reporting are errors, not fake news. Reputable news organizations—whether print, broadcast, or online—sometimes make mistakes. Factual errors do find their way into news reports from even the most respected news organizations. When alerted to errors, reputable publications, broadcasters, and online media will publicly correct them. Biased reporting is not fake news either. It is biased reporting. Some news media slant their stories to support a specific point of view. This can be done by highlighting some facts and omitting others, by quoting one source and not another, or by a variety of other means. Satire is another style of writing that has been confused with fake news. Although satire might be misunderstood or poorly done, it is not meant to be perceived as a factual account of events. Satire is a form of commentary, often on political or other topical issues. Through the use of humor, irony, or exaggeration, satire is meant to ridicule or criticize stupidity, vice, or societal flaws.

Who Produces Fake News?

Fake news comes from a variety of sources. Sometimes, it begins on websites that are created for the sole purpose of circulating made-up and misleading articles. Often, the creators of these websites deliberately choose website names and URLs that resemble those of legitimate news organizations. For example, websites like BostonTribune.com, KMT11.com, and ABCNews.com.co all sound like official, reputable news sources. Yet according to PolitiFact, a nonpartisan fact-checking website, all of these websites produce fake news stories, either by creating the content themselves or sharing it from other questionable sources. Frequently, readers who are casually scanning headlines and articles do not realize that the site they are looking at is not an actual news site.

Many fake news websites that emerged during the lead-up to the 2016 US elections have been traced to a small town in Macedonia, a country in southeastern Europe. Investigations by

BuzzFeed and *The Guardian* newspaper uncovered that more than one hundred fake news websites were run by a group of Macedonian teenagers. They did not care that the articles they posted were untrue. Nineteen-year-old Goran, a university student and one of the fake news producers, was interviewed by the British Broadcasting Corporation (BBC) in 2016. In the interview, Goran said it did not matter to him that the stories were false. "The Americans loved our stories and we make money from them," he says. "Who cares if they are true or false?"[12]

> "The Americans loved our stories and we make money from them. Who cares if they are true or false?"[12]
>
> —Goran, a Macedonian teen who spread fake news on social media during 2016

Driving Motivations

Like many other creators and distributors of fake news, Goran was in it for the money. Money is one of the top reasons why people create and distribute fake news. News articles—both real and fake—that spread on social media can earn significant amounts of money from advertising. When readers click on a headline, the link sends them to a website with paid advertisements. Sometimes, the website charges a set rate for running an ad. Other times the website collects money from the advertiser every time a user clicks on the ad. Either way, a website that gets a lot of hits can earn a lot of money.

This is how Goran earned his money. He explains that he often plagiarized fake news stories from other sites and reposted them on his websites with catchy new headlines. Then he paid Facebook to boost his posts on the newsfeeds of a target US audience so that more people saw them. When US Facebook users clicked on his fake stories, shared them, and liked them, Goran earned revenue from the advertising that appeared on his websites. In only one month, he earned about 1,800 euros ($2,061). Several of his friends earned thousands of euros per day. Goran is not concerned that his fake stories may have influenced American voters. "Teenagers in our city don't care how Americans vote," he says. "They are only satisfied that they make money and can buy expensive clothes and drinks!"[13]

American Paul Horner has also made money from fake news—earning as much as $10,000 per month in advertising revenue. In a 2016 interview with *Rolling Stone* magazine, he explained how he works. First, he makes up a story, such as this one: "Amish in America Commit Their Vote to Donald Trump." Then he posts the headline on Facebook. When readers click on the headline, the link drives them to one of his eight websites that has paid advertising. "Most of my stuff," he says, "starts off, the first paragraph is super legit, the title is super legit, the picture is super legit, but then the story just gets more and more

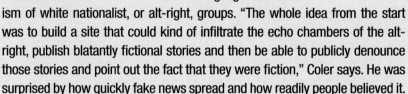

A Fake News Empire

Jestin Coler is a forty-year-old husband and father living in California. He is also a creator of fake news. In 2013 Coler got into fake news because he wanted to highlight the extremism of white nationalist, or alt-right, groups. "The whole idea from the start was to build a site that could kind of infiltrate the echo chambers of the alt-right, publish blatantly fictional stories and then be able to publicly denounce those stories and point out the fact that they were fiction," Coler says. He was surprised by how quickly fake news spread and how readily people believed it.

When fake news really took off in 2016, Coler's business did too. Today he employs twenty to twenty-five writers at any given time. As their stories spread across the Internet, Coler makes money from ads on his twenty-five websites. Although he declines to give a specific amount, he says that his fake news income ranges from $10,000 to $30,000 per month. Still, Coler insists that he does not do it for the money. "I do enjoy making a mess of the people that share the content that comes out of our site. It's not just the financial incentive for me. I still enjoy the game I guess."

Quoted in Laura Sydell, "We Tracked Down a Fake-News Creator in the Suburbs. Here's What We Learned," *All Tech Considered*, NPR, November 23, 2016. www.npr.org.

ridiculous and it becomes obvious that none of it is true." Thinking his stories are real, gullible or inattentive readers share them with people who share them again and again until they go viral. "It usually takes a couple of days," he says. "What I do is what I call 're-dating.' I keep putting it out there, day after day, changing the date of the story to match the current day. That makes it look brand new, like it just happened, which makes it keep going more and more viral."[14]

Money is not the only motivation for fake news. Some of the people who fabricate and distribute stories do so for ideological or political reasons. Their goal is to influence and manipulate people's opinions and behavior on political issues and elections. For example, the Romanian man who created the fake news site EndingtheFed.com explains that he launched the website mainly to support Donald Trump's 2016 campaign for president. He appreciated Trump's views on globalization, immigration, and trade. "In October 2015, I heard about Donald J. Trump and I liked him," he says. "I liked the fact that he is an outsider. I

Politics and ideology have played a role in the creation of fake news websites and the distribution of fabricated stories. According to US intelligence agencies, this was the motivation of outside entities seeking to ensure the election of Donald Trump as president.

studied him and the media. And I thought I can help him to win the presidency by creating a website."[15] The website ran fake stories under headlines such as "It's Over: Hillary's ISIS Email Just Leaked & It's Worse than Anyone Could Have Imagined" and "Just Read the Law: Hillary Is Disqualified from Holding Any Federal Office."[16] According to BuzzFeed, this site was responsible for four of the top ten fake election stories with the most engagement on social media.

A Real Problem

In recent years, fake news has become a real problem. Across the world, social media use is rising sharply. Unlike older media technologies, social media content can be uploaded by anyone with an Internet connection and shared with millions of users without any third party filtering, fact-checking, or editing. Using the power of social media, a single user can upload content that can reach as many readers as traditional media like the *New York Times*. According to Zoe Hawkins, an analyst who researches international and domestic cyber policy issues at the Australian Strategic Policy Institute's International Cyber Policy Centre,

> The rise of the blogger, vlogger and tweeter has made everyone a journalist and sparked a boom in content creation by the general public. The transition from traditional media to lower threshold information sharing means there's been a proliferation of opinions published online—a great thing for freedom of expression. Unfortunately, this has created significant noise around important issues, [and has] diluted the credibility of news on many newsfeeds.[17]

The most serious impact of fake news is its ability to influence people's views and votes. When fake news abounds before an election, it can affect attitudes toward candidates and issues and cause people to vote a certain way or not vote at all. This, says

Hawkins, is a threat to the integrity of elections and democracies. She explains:

> The power of cyberspace to influence the democratic process lies in much more than just the nuts and bolts of the election infrastructure. Every vote cast on election day is the product of the information ecosystem of the preceding months. Shaping the nature and volume of information available to the public in the lead-up to an election is a sophisticated way of influencing voter decision-making and election outcomes. In this method of tampering with elections, a culprit's digital fingerprints can never be directly linked to the election per se. Election decision-making can be influenced through the dissemination of "fake news" or "strategic disclosures," and the impact of this false or previously unavailable information can be increased through the creation of an "artificial consensus" online.[18]

A Loss of Trust

Fake news can become a serious problem when real-world resources are misallocated because of false information. For example, during the chaos after the 2013 Boston Marathon bombing, the Massachusetts Institute of Technology (MIT) campus was locked down. During the lockdown, MIT professor Sinan Aral was on the campus. "Information was scarce, and we didn't know which parts of campus were safe," he says. "We turned to Twitter for updates and found that in addition to the true breaking news, which was more up-to-date than any television broadcasts, a lot of false information was spreading and misdirecting law enforcement. If attackers know that law enforcement relies on social media, they can use it to proactively thwart police responses."[19]

Fake news and misinformation can also affect the real world financially. In 2013, one fake tweet claiming that President Barack Obama had been injured in an explosion caused a $130 billion drop in stock value in a single day. Although stock prices recovered shortly after the tweet was proved to be false, the experience showed how vulnerable the financial markets can be to fake news. "If you can lower the price of a stock by one percent by purposefully manipulating the news flow by producing content and if you have the right trading mechanism in place, you can capitalize on that," says Anton Gordon, the cofounder of Indexer.me in Houston, a software developer that builds algorithms to determine the reliability of text and visual content. "Imagine if you can recognize that the story is not the least bit credible and you know the stock will recover, you can really capitalize on that knowledge."[20]

In 2017 Starbucks was the victim of fake news when tweets promoting "Dreamer Day" promised that the coffee chain was giving free Frappuccinos to undocumented immigrants in the United States. The false promise spread quickly online and included real touches, like the company's logo, signature font, and pictures of its drinks. Concerned about damage to the company's public image and brand, Starbucks quickly denied the story and turned to Twitter to clarify that it had been completely made up.

Fake news has the power to disrupt business, politics, and even emergency response efforts. The greatest damage, however, may be to trust. In a democracy, citizens must be able to trust the people who represent them in government, the institutions (such as the news media) that inform them, and the entities (such as businesses) that provide them with all sorts of items and services. Brooke Binkowski, the managing editor of the fact-checking website Snopes, comments that fake news threatens businesses, but her comments can be applied even more broadly to the American way of life: "It hurts businesses financially and it also makes things toxic for them by destroying trust and creating an atmosphere in which people don't know who they can trust."[21]

> "It hurts businesses financially and it also makes things toxic for them by destroying trust and creating an atmosphere in which people don't know who they can trust."[21]
>
> —Brooke Binkowski, the managing editor of the fact-checking website Snopes

CHAPTER TWO

Why Is Fake News So Hard to Spot?

When North Carolina truck driver Chris Gromek wants to learn the latest news, he scans the Internet and satellite radio. He no longer turns to television news networks such as MSNBC and Fox News because he believes they present conflicting—and sometimes false—reports that are skewed by politics. "Where is the truth?"[22] asks Gromek.

Like Gromek, many Americans are increasingly confused about what media sources can be trusted to report the truth. Many people seek out various sources of information and often trust a few in particular. "It has made me take every story with a large grain, a block of salt," says Lori Viars, an Ohio resident. "Not just from liberal sources. I've seen conservative 'fake news.'"[23] A 2016 Pew Research Center poll found that 64 percent of American adults believe that fake news has resulted in a great deal of confusion about current events and political issues. Additionally, 23 percent said they had shared fake news themselves—both by mistake and intentionally.

Many Americans express confidence about being able to spot fake news. In a survey released in 2018 by the *Economist* newspaper and global public opinion firm YouGov, 70 percent of those surveyed said they were at least somewhat confident they could tell the difference between real news and fake news, with 28 percent saying they were very confident. And yet, as indicated by the Pew poll (and others that have been done since), the public continues to be taken in by fake websites and fabricated stories.

Experts say that several factors contribute to this confusion. One factor may be the sheer volume of information available online from mainstream media sources, Internet sources, and social media. "I think part of the problem is that now people are getting too much information and it confuses them and they don't know how to decipher the true and the fake,"[24] says Trent Lott, a former Republican senator from Mississippi. Adding to the problem, many fake news creators intentionally design their websites and articles to resemble legitimate sites and stories. Additionally, the increasing misuse of the *fake news* label, the misunderstanding of satirical articles, and the spread of rumor and gossip online also make it harder to identify fake news.

> "I think part of the problem is that now people are getting too much information and it confuses them and they don't know how to decipher the true and the fake."[24]
>
> —Trent Lott, a former Senate Republican leader from Mississippi

Poll results show that many Americans believe they can tell the difference between legitimate news stories and fabricated ones. And yet the public continues to be fooled by fake websites and false news and information.

Experts agree that it can be difficult to identify which stories are true and which are fake. "In today's world, nobody can tell for sure that the information they receive is 100 percent accurate and reliable," says Janey Lee, an assistant professor of journalism at Lehigh University in Bethlehem, Pennsylvania. "Even experts have a hard time weeding out fake accounts and automatic messages."[25]

Designed to Deceive

Fake news is often hard to identify because its creators want it to be mistaken for truthful reporting. The point is to confuse people into thinking that they are looking at trusted sources and factual stories. Everything about these sites is intended to confuse users, starting with site names that are often only one or two letters different from a real news organization. According to PolitiFact, ABCNews.com.co, for example, is a fake news site that has often been confused with ABCNews.com, which is the web address of the mainstream ABC News network. Not surprisingly, the fake site has the look and feel of the real site—which adds to the confusion.

It is not just the site name that confuses users. The articles themselves often appear to be legitimate. Fake news producers write headlines that sound plausible, especially to people who want to believe them. Often, creators take a small piece of truthful information that sounds accurate and make up details to build a story around it. These false stories spread like wildfire across the Internet, being posted and shared by readers on a variety of platforms, which makes it difficult to trace back to a single website. In December 2016, shortly after Donald Trump's election as president, stories spread across the Internet that liberal Supreme Court justice Ruth Bader Ginsburg had announced her retirement. Dozens of websites ran stories that cited an Associated Press interview in which Ginsburg supposedly said she could not imagine serving as a justice under Trump. The fake articles were designed to look real. They even began with a quote from an actual Associated Press interview with Ginsburg in which she voiced her opinion of candidate Trump. However, that interview had taken place months before the November presidential election. The quote used in the fake stories was taken out of context, and supporting details were fabricated to make it seem as though Ginsburg were about to retire.

In 2018 fake news stories appeared online claiming that social media giant Facebook had hired George Soros, a billionaire investor known for funding liberal causes, to remove unwanted conservative content from the social network in order to better regulate elections. In reality, Facebook announced in May 2018 that it was

Online stories circulating in 2016 claimed that liberal US Supreme Court justice Ruth Bader Ginsburg had announced her retirement from the high court. The stories were false, but bits of real interviews interspersed with made-up information made the stories seem credible.

partnering with the Atlantic Council, an American think tank, to help it reduce the flow of misinformation during election periods around the world. Although one of Soros's philanthropic organizations was among those that had donated to the Atlantic Council in previous years, Soros was not a member of the think tank's board of directors nor was he affiliated with the council. The fake stories exaggerated and mischaracterized the connection between Soros and Facebook and made up additional details. Even though it was deemed false by FactCheck.org, the false news gathered thousands of likes, shares, and comments on the social network.

Overuse of the Fake News Label

Further blurring the line between truth and fiction, the phrase *fake news* has been used to describe all sorts of news and information, regardless of the quality of the reporting or the soundness of the information. President Trump is perhaps the most famous—and most frequent—user of this label. According to a CNN report, Trump used the word *fake* more than four hundred times during his first year as president to describe a variety of information sources including polls, media, and stories. In a February 6, 2017, tweet, for instance, Trump wrote, "Any negative polls are fake news, just like the CNN, ABC, NBC polls in the election."[26]

Critics say that Trump uses the term to discredit news reports that he disagrees with or finds unflattering. And polls show that this strategy might be working. A June 2018 poll by news and information website Axios and SurveyMonkey found that 72 percent of respondents believe that traditional major news outlets report stories that they know to be false or misleading. Nearly two-thirds of those polled said that they believed fake news was reported because the journalists and news outlets had a political or ideological agenda. Media watchers say that overuse of the term *fake news* by Trump and other prominent people is adding to confusion among members of the public and represents a danger to a valued piece of American life. In August 2018 news

Cognitive Dissonance

At first glance, some fake news stories seem too absurd to be believable. Headlines such as "Miami-Dade to Create Freeway 'Texting Lane' to Accommodate Millennial Drivers" and "Republicans to Institute Saliva Tests to Determine If Poor People Are Hungry Before They Can Use Food Stamps" might seem silly, but then why do so many people fall for fake news stories like these? The answer, according to some experts, may be partially linked to cognitive dissonance. Cognitive dissonance occurs in situations where a person experiences conflicting attitudes, beliefs, or behaviors. For example, people who smoke but also know that smoking causes cancer face an internal conflict. They are in a state of cognitive dissonance. Cognitive dissonance creates a feeling of discomfort that leads them to change their attitudes, beliefs, or behaviors to reduce the discomfort. If they read a fake news article that claims smoking does not cause cancer or any other health problems, they feel better about their habit. When they see the same information repeated on social media, they believe it must be true. In this way, they can minimize the unhealthy effects of cigarettes and continue to feel good about smoking. Their internal conflict is resolved.

Vikram Bhoyrul, "7 of the Craziest Fake News Stories," ITP Live, March 14, 2017. www.itpliveme.com.

media around the country ran editorials making this point. An editorial that appeared in the *New York Times* stated,

> Criticizing the news media—for underplaying or overplaying stories, for getting something wrong—is entirely right. News reporters and editors are human, and make mistakes. Correcting them is core to our job. But insisting that truths you don't like are "fake news" is dangerous to the lifeblood of democracy. And calling journalists the "enemy of the people" is dangerous, period.[27]

Other people in the spotlight have also used the *fake news* label to cast doubt on unfavorable news reports. In 2018 Brigadier

General Kurt Stein of the US Marine Corps said he considered allegations of sexual harassment under his command to be fake news. The allegations, which were first reported by *USA Today* in February 2018, were made by two civilian employees who said that a Marine Corps officer had sexually harassed them. At the time that Stein called the allegations fake news, they were still under investigation by the Marines. After his superiors learned of his comments, the Marines suspended Stein.

Discrediting the Opposition

In countries controlled by dictators and autocrats, the *fake news* label is being used to discredit opposition parties and candidates and to dismiss criticism and legitimate grievances. For instance, a detailed 2017 Amnesty International report accused Syria of hanging as many as thirteen thousand prisoners without trial during that

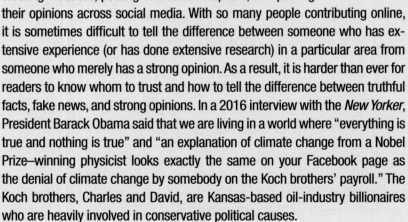

Everyone Is an Expert

In the digital age, anyone with a computer and an Internet connection can upload content. People are writing blogs, creating websites, posting entries to Wikipedia, and posting their opinions across social media. With so many people contributing online, it is sometimes difficult to tell the difference between someone who has extensive experience (or has done extensive research) in a particular area from someone who merely has a strong opinion. As a result, it is harder than ever for readers to know whom to trust and how to tell the difference between truthful facts, fake news, and strong opinions. In a 2016 interview with the *New Yorker*, President Barack Obama said that we are living in a world where "everything is true and nothing is true" and "an explanation of climate change from a Nobel Prize–winning physicist looks exactly the same on your Facebook page as the denial of climate change by somebody on the Koch brothers' payroll." The Koch brothers, Charles and David, are Kansas-based oil-industry billionaires who are heavily involved in conservative political causes.

Quoted in Casey Newton, "Obama Criticizes the Spread of Fake News on Facebook," Verge, November 17, 2016. www.theverge.com.

country's civil war. When asked about the report, Syrian president Bashar al-Assad dismissed it as false, saying, "We're living in a fake-news era, as you know."[28]

With the phrase *fake news* being applied to an ever-expanding list of items—including false reports, misinformation, biased reporting, conspiracy theories, mistakes, satire, and reporting that people simply don't like—the meaning has become murky. "We did this to ourselves, and by 'we,' I mean the media," says Alexios Mantzarlis, director of the International Fact-Checking Network at the Poynter Institute, a nonprofit journalism school. He suggests that the media bears some responsibility in the overuse and misuse of the label. "Right after the election, in editorials, in news articles, we started calling 'fake news' a bit of everything. We should be conscious that our industry is partly to blame for the confusion we're at."[29] For that reason, some journalism experts are trying not to use the term *fake news* at all. "The reason I don't like the phrase now is it's used as a term to describe everything," says Clare Wardle of First Draft News, a truth-seeking nonprofit based at Harvard University's Shorenstein Center. "Whether it's a sponsored post, an ad, a visual meme, a bot on Twitter, a rumor—people just use it against any information they don't like. This is a really complex problem," she says. "If we're going to start thinking of ways we can intervene, we're going to have to have clear definitions."[30]

> "We did this to ourselves, and by 'we,' I mean the media. Right after the election, in editorials, in news articles, we started calling 'fake news' a bit of everything. We should be conscious that our industry is partly to blame for the confusion we're at."[29]
>
> —Alexios Mantzarlis, the director of the Poynter Institute's International Fact-Checking Network

Misunderstanding Satirical Content

Satirical websites and articles have also become part of the confusion over fake news. Satire is the use of humor, sarcasm, irony, or exaggeration to expose an individual's, group's, or institution's flaws. Satire has traditionally offered people a way to comment on and criticize ideas, events, and actions—especially those involving public figures and institutions. This type of writing often uses humor, although humor with an edge, to entertain readers. One of the most well-known contemporary producers of satire is a website called the Onion. Most of the site's content is fairly absurd, such as a September 2018 headline which reads, "Cash-Strapped Zuckerberg Forced to Sell 11 Million Facebook Users."[31]

Although many people understand that the Onion and other websites offer satirical content, many others do not. Increasingly, satire is being confused with factual reporting. Sometimes, this occurs when casual readers quickly scan headlines or the first paragraph of a story that appears online. Then, thinking the story is factual, they share it on social media—often with comments expressing their outrage. Anger builds as the story—which was never intended to be taken as fact—is shared again and again as confirmation of some preconceived idea of attitudes or behavior.

Other times, the confusion appears to be intentional. In June 2017 a story about Republican senator and House speaker Paul Ryan began circulating on the Internet and social media. It first appeared on Politicot.com, which claims to be a purveyor of satire. But critics have wondered publicly if the site deals in satire or fake news. To begin with, its name is remarkably similar to an actual news site called Politico.com—which could be confusing from the start. The story in question quoted Ryan as saying that "22 million Americans choose to be poor, so it's their own problem if they can't afford to be healthy."[32] Ryan never actually said this. But the story began with a factual paragraph, followed by all sorts of made-up supporting details that led many people to believe that they were reading a news story (rather than a satirical one).

Falling for Fake News

Because there is a lot of confusion about what is real and what is fake online, it is not surprising that many people admit to being duped by fake news at one time or another. In Florida, Lake

A Florida school board member admitted that he was duped by fabricated stories claiming that mass shooting survivor David Hogg (being interviewed) was a paid actor rather than a student at Marjorie Stoneman Douglas High School.

County School Board member Bill Mathias admits that he was fooled by fake news in 2018. After the 2018 school shootings at Marjory Stoneman Douglas High School, high school student David Hogg made several appearances on local and national media outlets to talk about the shooting. False information began to circulate online that Hogg was not a student at the high school but rather a paid crisis actor—that is, a trained actor who is paid to play the role of a disaster victim during emergency training drills. Although the information was false, it spread widely across social media, even landing on Mathias's Facebook page. "It said that he was a 'crisis actor,' and I had 'Googled' him first, because there is responsibility with the fake news to try and validate," says Mathias, "and the first things come up all say he's a crisis actor, so I shared it." Once he realized that the post was fake news, Mathias deleted it from his Facebook page. "I saw that, in fact, he is a student. I took it down and posted what was the truth and said I was incorrect about it."[33]

Ohio State University researchers have examined data from three national surveys to better understand how people form beliefs and how that might affect their willingness to accept fake news. Their 2017 report found that people who trust their intuition or believe the facts they hear are shaped by political bias are more likely to believe fake news. Others, who rely more on concrete evidence to form beliefs, are less likely to believe fake news. "While trusting your gut may be beneficial in some situations, it turns out that putting faith in intuition over evidence leaves us susceptible to misinformation,"[34] says study coauthor Brian Weeks.

As false and misleading information floods news feeds, Internet sites, and media outlets, people are becoming more confused about what to believe and what sources to trust. Media experts who have studied fake news suggest that people should look at everything they read and watch with a certain level of healthy skepticism. "Part of what we have to do ourselves is to create an internal speed bump, where we say, 'Just wait a minute' before you believe anything,"[35] says Dan Gillmor, a professor at Arizona State University's Walter Cronkite School of Journalism and Mass Communication. He also suggests that people seek out reliable news organizations and rely on them more than unfamiliar sources which may or may not be credible. Doing so may make it easier for people to identify fake news for what it truly is—a piece of fiction.

CHAPTER THREE

Social Media's Role in the Spread of Fake News

Without social media and the Internet, would fake news be the issue it is today? The answer is probably not. That is not to say it would not exist. "The spread of junk news is not a new phenomenon: tabloidization, false content, conspiracy theories and political propaganda all have histories. But social media has drastically changed the scale and speed at which junk news is distributed and consumed,"[36] write researchers Samantha Bradshaw and Philip N. Howard in a 2018 paper on media and democracy. If the Internet is the superhighway for the spread of fake news, social media is the vehicle that speeds it from one place to another.

A Powerful Tool

In a very short time, social media has become extremely powerful in spreading information. Founded in 2004, Facebook has more than 2 billion monthly active users around the world. That is more than the population of any nation on the planet. In fact, nearly 30 percent of the world's 7.6 billion people are Facebook users. While not as big as Facebook, other popular social media sites have their own powerful reach. In 2018 YouTube had approximately 1.9 billion active users worldwide, WhatsApp had 1.5 billion users, and Twitter had 335 million active users.

Social media sites have become a major source of news and information for many people. These sites do not generate or distribute news. Rather, users get updates, stories, images, and videos from news outlets, organizations, companies, and celebrities

Social media has become a powerful tool for the spread of news and information. Users get updates, stories, images, and videos from the news outlets, organizations, companies, and celebrities they follow, or see them as they are shared by other users.

that they follow on social media, or see them as they are shared by other users. According to a 2017 Pew Research survey, about two-thirds of American adults get a portion of their news through social media, with 20 percent doing so often. Facebook tops the list of social media news sources, followed by YouTube, and then Twitter. According to the Pew survey, 45 percent of American adults get news through their Facebook page. One reason social media is such a popular source of news is because it is so easy to use. Anyone can post status updates, give opinions, like posts and tweets, and share content. However, because the sites themselves have traditionally done little, if any, vetting of content, it is just as easy to share a falsehood as it is to share a fact. As a result, few safeguards have existed to help users distinguish between facts and fiction online.

Because of social media's powerful reach, the repercussions of spreading false information can be significant. For example, in March 2018 President Donald Trump tweeted about e-commerce giant Amazon, "I have stated my concerns with Amazon long before the Election. Unlike others, they pay little or no taxes to state & local governments, use our Postal System as their Delivery Boy (causing tremendous loss to the U.S.), and are putting many thousands of retailers out of business!"[37] He followed up in early April with an additional tweet accusing the company of taking advantage of the US Postal Service and costing taxpayers billions of dollars. In the weeks after the tweets, Amazon's stock price dropped 7 percent, causing a loss of billions of dollars in the company's stock. Although Trump's tweets were inaccurate—Amazon, in fact, does collect sales taxes from consumers in forty-five states and the District of Columbia, and those taxes are sent to local and state taxing agencies—the episode illustrates the power of social media to have real-world effects.

Fake News Spreads More Quickly

Social media's growing dominance as a source of news and information led researchers at MIT to wonder about the speed at which false news travels. Their study, published in the journal *Science* in 2018, found that falsehoods actually spread faster and wider over social media than the truth. "It took the truth about six times as long as falsehood to reach 1,500 people,"[38] the researchers write.

Study leader Soroush Vosoughi became interested in this topic when he noticed how rapidly false reports spread on Twitter after the 2013 Boston Marathon bombings. As police hunted for the bombers, Vosoughi and millions of other Boston residents were asked to stay in their homes. At the time, "Twitter became our main source of news," Vosoughi says. "I realized that . . . a good chunk of what I was reading on social media was rumors."[39] In the study, the MIT researchers examined 126,000

> "It took the truth about six times as long as falsehood to reach 1,500 people."[38]
>
> —MIT researchers studying fake news

stories that were tweeted by 3 million people more than 4.5 million times. They discovered that false news stories were 70 percent more likely to be retweeted than factual reports. In addition, the false stories stuck around longer, carrying into more unbroken retweet chains.

The MIT study focused on *what* was occurring but did not examine *why* it was occurring. Some experts have suggested an explanation. They note that fabricated stories are often more provocative, unusual, and interesting than factual information—and that is the appeal. They attract attention and stoke the urge to share. "False news is more novel, and people are more likely to share novel information,"[40] says Sinan Aral, another researcher who has studied the spread of fake news on social media.

> **"False news is more novel, and people are more likely to share novel information."[40]**
>
> —Sinan Aral, a researcher who has studied the spread of fake news

A simple tweet by a Texas man shows how easy it is for fake news to go viral on social media. On November 9, 2016, Eric Tucker noticed a large group of buses near downtown Austin, Texas. He also heard reports of protests against Trump, who had just won the presidential election. Tucker connected the two and posted pictures of the buses on his Twitter account with the comment, "Anti-Trump protestors in Austin today are not as organic as they seem. Here are the busses they came in. #fakeprotests #trump2016 #austin."[41]

Tucker admits that he did not try to confirm the accuracy of his assumption that the buses were related to anti-Trump protests. In fact, the buses were in town for a business conference. "I did think in the back of my mind there could be other explanations, but it just didn't seem plausible,"[42] he said in an interview. Tucker also noted that because he had only forty Twitter followers, he did not think his tweet would be seen by many people. Several hours later, though, Tucker's tweet was posted on Reddit, where it generated hundreds of comments. By the next morning, other

Living in a Filter Bubble

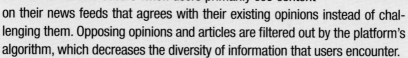

Social media's ability to personalize what content users see based on their likes and preferences also creates a filter bubble. A filter bubble occurs when users primarily see content on their news feeds that agrees with their existing opinions instead of challenging them. Opposing opinions and articles are filtered out by the platform's algorithm, which decreases the diversity of information that users encounter.

When users are surrounded by people and information that already agree with their views, it strengthens their confirmation bias. Confirmation bias makes it more likely for them to believe information that matches their existing beliefs. As a result, they spend little time attempting to confirm it. At the same time, when new information opposes existing beliefs, they are more likely to discard it as fake, whether it is or not. Confirmation bias affects the ability to process information and determine whether it is true or false. It is one of the reasons why many people can easily spot fake news when they do not agree with it, but fall for it when it supports their point of view.

social media accounts linked to the post. By the morning of November 10, Tucker's initial Twitter post had been retweeted and liked more than five thousand times. Later that day, conservative blogs posted stories that incorporated Tucker's tweet and photos, calling him an eyewitness in Austin. On November 11, local television and newspapers reported that the buses were in town for the business conference, and Tucker tweeted that he might have been wrong. Still, his initial tweet continued to be shared thousands of times on Facebook and other social media sites.

Disinformation After a Disaster

The ability of social media to reach a large number of people very quickly is not always bad. When a public emergency occurs (for example, a terrorist attack, a wildfire, or flooding) social media can be used to get lifesaving information to a lot of people in a very short time. In Florida, first responders and government officials used social media to communicate and coordinate their efforts during Hurricane Irma in 2017. Florida's tourism office sent targeted messages on Facebook to nearly three hundred thousand people believed to be visiting the area, warning them to take precautions. Governor Rick Scott worked with Google to make sure Google Maps quickly updated for road closures because of the storm. The National Oceanic and Atmospheric Administration used Twitter to post frequent updates about the path of the storm.

However, social media can also be used to spread fake news and disinformation, which can disrupt efforts to help people in need and cause additional distress for those who have already experienced a traumatic event. In the hours after a March 2017 terror attack killed six people and injured dozens more in London, some people searching for missing loved ones turned to social media. They posted photos, hoping that someone in the area had information on their whereabouts. However, several of the photos were fake, mainly posted by users hoping to generate more retweets and activity on their social media accounts. For example, one Twitter user posted a photo of someone she claimed was her younger brother. She said he had Down syndrome. The photo turned out to be a fake. The fake post received seventeen thousand retweets.

In a study published in 2018, researchers at the University at Buffalo examined how good Twitter's most active users were at detecting fake news during public emergencies. They examined more than twenty thousand tweets made during Hurricane Sandy in 2012 and the Boston Marathon bombing in 2013. They looked at four false rumors—two from the marathon and two from the hurricane—and examined what Twitter users did with the false information. Users generally handled it in three main ways: they tried to confirm the information, they spread it without question, or they cast doubt upon it. The researchers found that 86 to 91 percent of users spread the false news by retweeting it or liking it. Only 5 to 9 percent of users attempted to confirm the news, often by retweeting it and asking if it was accurate. Between 1 and 9 percent cast doubt on the original false tweet, often saying that it was not accurate.

In the immediate chaos that followed the 2013 Boston Marathon bombing, many people turned to Twitter for updates and information. One researcher later determined that falsehoods were retweeted far more often than factual reports.

Even after the information had proved to be false, less than 10 percent of the users who spread the fake news deleted their retweets, and less than 20 percent sent out a new tweet to correct the information in the false retweet. "These findings are important because they show how easily people are deceived during times when they are most vulnerable and the role social media platforms play in these deceptions,"[43] says the study's lead author, Jun Zhuang, an associate professor in the university's School of Engineering and Applied Sciences. However, although Twitter users were more likely to spread fake news during a disaster, the researchers found that the social media platforms themselves often moved quickly to correct any fake news items on their networks as soon as they discovered them.

Algorithms

Why does fake news spread so quickly on social media? One reason might be how social media platforms work. They rely on

algorithms to deliver news and other content to their users. An algorithm is a process or set of rules followed by a computer in a calculation or other problem-solving operation. Social media's complex algorithms sort, filter, and deliver content in order to maximize a user's engagement with the content. For example, Facebook's January 2018 algorithm update puts content that receives the most engagement—measured in reactions, comments, and shares—the highest on a user's feed. Facebook also tracks a user's personal engagement with friends' posts and brand pages. Depending on the user's settings, the Facebook news feed algorithm uses these personal interactions to calculate what a user wants to see on his or her feed, putting similar posts higher on the feed. Search algorithms are a key part of the social media experience. Without them, users would have to sort through massive amounts of information in which they have little interest.

The way social media algorithms select content and personalize search results enables the spread of fake news. By selecting content that is personalized to what a user already likes, it limits the flow of new information. Instead of humans selecting truthful sources of news and information to be placed in news feeds, complex computer algorithms select what information is delivered and what is excluded. Popular content, measured by the number of likes or engagement, is more likely to appear, regardless of whether it is factual or fake. The more users engage with content, the faster it spreads to more people. Fake news goes viral. At the same time, social media's algorithms, which prioritize content based on interests and past behavior, make it more difficult for users to find news and information that may have a different viewpoint.

Advertising

Social media's advertising model also contributes to the spread of fake news. Social media platforms earn money by collecting user data and selling it to third parties. Companies buy user information because it helps them understand the interests and desires of large populations of users. With this understanding, they can identify which users might be most likely to buy their products or services and create targeted advertising messages for those specific groups. Then, using social media's algorithms, they can deliver these targeted ads to the right people at the right time.

This advertising model contributes to the spread of fake news in two ways. First, it rewards content that goes viral. This incentive has led to an increase in what are known as clickbait headlines, which are designed to entice users to click through to a certain website or video. Clickbait headlines often purposely provide just enough information to spark curiosity or outrage so that a reader wants to click through to the linked content. When they reach the article, the webpage also features ads, each of which has paid to

be there. At the same time, all those clicks count as engagement on the social media site, driving up the popularity of the fake news in the platform's algorithm, making it more likely to be shown on news feeds.

Social media's ability to target advertising to specific groups of users with desired characteristics also contributes to the spread of fake news. Fake news creators target specific groups of voters with targeted messages designed to influence their opinion about political candidates and issues. "Overall, the way in which advertising takes place on social media can exacerbate not only the scale of fake news and misinformation, but enhance its effectiveness by reaching audiences with messages that appeal to their psychoanalytical profiles based on a user's online actions,"[44] write Bradshaw and Howard.

Manipulating Social Media

Those who wish to manipulate public opinion and spread fake news can use algorithms and advertising to do so. Using a variety of strategies, they seek to take advantage of each platform's unique workings. On Facebook, for example, the platform's algorithm is driven by engagement. Posts with a lot of likes, shares, and comments are more likely to appear in news feeds. Manipulators can set up numerous fake Facebook accounts to add likes and shares to increase a post's engagement, pushing it higher in the platform's algorithm. On Twitter, manipulators want to make a fake news story appear to have been retweeted by as many users as possible. The more it is retweeted, the higher it appears in the Twitter search system, which makes it more likely to be retweeted again.

Manipulating social media to spread fake news often means using a combination of fake accounts and an army of automated bots, which are software applications that run automated tasks on the Internet like posting, liking, or retweeting on social media. Ben Nimmo, a defense and international security analyst with the Atlantic Council's Digital Forensic Research Lab, has followed the spread of fake news and the trolls who use automated bots to spread propaganda on social media. Propaganda has traditionally been associated with governments. Governments have been known to engage in misinformation campaigns to help convince citizens that their actions are

> "The goal of a propagandist is to spread your message, and the best way to do that is to get people to do it for you. You can't tell a million people what to do. You need to get 10 people, and they spread it [en masse]."[45]
>
> —Ben Nimmo, a defense and international security analyst with the Atlantic Council's Digital Forensic Research Lab

just or for the good of the nation. These days, the term is often used to describe any individual or group engaged in spreading false information. "The goal of a propagandist is to spread your message, and the best way to do that is to get people to do it for you," says Nimmo. "You can't tell a million people what to do. You need to get 10 people, and they spread it [en masse]."[45]

Nimmo describes a typical process that takes place in three stages. First, so-called shepherd accounts, which are run by highly active and influential people, kick off a trending topic. These accounts can be fake, such as a Russian account disguised as a conservative group in Tennessee. The shepherd accounts tweet or post and express outrage over a fake news article. Next, "sheepdog" accounts, which are run by people affiliated with the shepherd, follow and retweet the content and add comments to give the appearance of real engagement. Finally, "sheep" accounts, which are automated bots, add artificial retweets and likes, dramatically increasing the post's engagement. Thousands of retweets can trick casual users into believing that the fake article is real. Although this type of attack does not always work, it can cause fake news topics to trend on social media along with legitimate stories.

Fake news has long existed, but the arrival of social media has accelerated its spread and amplified its reach to people all over the world. To fight the spread of fake news, social media users must arm themselves with knowledge and bring a critical eye to everything they read online. By understanding how fake news spreads and the motivations behind it, users will be better able to detect it online.

CHAPTER FOUR

Election Interference

US elections have long been considered a shining example of democracy in action. In 2016 Americans learned that voters and elections are vulnerable to manipulation by outside forces. In February 2018 the US Justice Department charged thirteen people and three companies (all Russian) in a sophisticated plot to interfere in the 2016 US presidential election. The goal, prosecutors said, was to undermine Hillary Clinton's campaign and promote Donald Trump's campaign. One of the most prominent tactics employed by the Russians was the use of social media to manipulate public opinion. The indictment alleged that the Russians stole the identities of American citizens and then, using those identities, posed as political activists. They then posted news and opinions online, specifically on the highly charged issues of immigration, religion, and race. They sought to increase divisiveness and rancor in the American public. "The indictment alleges that the Russian conspirators want to promote discord in the United States and undermine public confidence in democracy," stated US deputy attorney general Rod Rosenstein in a news conference. "We must not allow them to succeed."[46]

As early as 2014, prosecutors allege, Russian computer specialists created hundreds of social media accounts that gathered hundreds of thousands of followers. They pretended to be Christian activists, supporters of the Black Lives Matter movement, and anti-immigration groups. "I created all these pictures and posts, and the Americans believed that it was written by their people,"[47] one of the Russians, Irina Viktorovna Kaverzina, wrote in an e-mail to a colleague. The Russians sought to hurt Clinton's campaign by getting more people to support her Democratic rival, Bernie Sanders. They stirred unrest by promoting allegations of Democratic voter fraud. They also staged political rallies across the country; they promoted these events on social media and used fake accounts to recruit volunteers. The Russians also bought political advertisements on social media that supported Trump and opposed Clinton. American intelligence officials have said that they have no way of knowing whether the Russian actions affected the outcome of the election.

In July 2018 Rosenstein announced additional charges related to Russian meddling in the 2016 election. A grand jury indicted twelve more Russians for allegedly hacking into US computer systems during the election. "The object of the conspiracy was to hack into the computers of U.S. persons and entities involved in the 2016 presidential election, steal documents from those computers, and stage releases of the stolen documents to interfere with the 2016 U.S. presidential election,"[48] the indictment read. Rosenstein stated that the defendants targeted volunteers and employees of Clinton's campaign. First, they tricked them into clicking on e-mails that included malware that enabled the Russians to steal their usernames and passwords. With this personal information, they were then able to hack into the computer networks of the Democratic National Campaign Committee and Democratic National Committee (DNC), where they stole thousands of private e-mails. The Russians then posted the stolen e-mails online during the period leading up to the election, hoping to influence public opinion and negatively portray Clinton and the DNC.

Influencing the Political Process

Previous elections were primarily a contest between political parties, each trying to get their message out to the public. To reach voters, the candidates and parties organized rallies and speeches, scheduled media interviews and appearances, bought advertisements, and paid for mailings. As in any election, the goal was to win voter support for specific candidates and positions. Although there have been complaints in some elections about ballot tampering and other issues, most elections in the United States have proceeded in straightforward fashion.

The Internet and social media have opened the door to other influences on US elections, however. From fake news and disinformation to outright hacking in order to steal and release damaging private information, those who want to manipulate US elections have gone online to interfere in ways not previously possible. "The vast majority of people . . . would be surprised at the extent

In 2016 Americans learned that their elections are vulnerable to manipulation. Various individuals and companies from Russia have been charged with trying to undermine Hillary Clinton's bid for president and promote Donald Trump's campaign.

to which these platforms are used for political manipulation. Especially with nobody doing anything about it,"[49] says Emilio Ferrara, a researcher at the University of Southern California.

Election interference is not just an American problem. In France in 2017, presidential candidate Emmanuel Macron and his political party, La République En Marche!, were the targets of a massive hacking attack hours before the French people were scheduled to vote. Hackers infiltrated private computer networks and stole tens of thousands of internal e-mails and other documents. An anonymous user called EMLEAKS posted this information, including some documents said to be false, on a document-sharing site called Pastebin. Within an hour of being posted online, a link to the leaked materials appeared on an online political discussion forum. From there, it was picked up by a reporter for a far-right Canadian outlet. The reporter posted a link to the forum on Twitter. The tweet went viral.

> "The vast majority of people . . . would be surprised at the extent to which these platforms are used for political manipulation. Especially with nobody doing anything about it."[49]
>
> —Emilio Ferrara, a researcher at the University of Southern California

The stolen data, according to party officials, included e-mails, accounting statements, and contracts stolen from the personal and professional accounts of some of the party's staff. "Coming in the final hours of the campaign, this operation clearly amounts to democratic destabilization," it said. La République En Marche! also accused the hackers of mixing many false documents in with the stolen ones on social media "in order to sow doubt and disinformation" as part of an operation "clearly intended to harm the movement."[50]

Earlier during the election campaign, Macron's campaign team had accused Russian interests of attempting to hack its computer systems and suspected they were also behind this latest hack. To date, Russia has denied any involvement in the hacks and election interference. Ultimately, the leaks did little to impact the election's outcome. Macron, leading in the polls before the leaks, won the election to become France's president.

A Common Practice

Although election interference made headlines in the United States in 2016 and in France in 2017, this sort of activity is not unique. According to a 2017 report from Oxford University's Computational Propaganda Research Project, online campaigns to manipulate public opinion and elections through false or misleading social media posts have become standard political practice around the world.

According to the report, cybertroops, which are government, military, or political party teams, are commonly organized to manipulate public opinion on political matters using social media. Interference affects dozens of countries worldwide and occurs on every social media platform, including Facebook, Twitter, Instagram, and more. "We find that cyber troops are a pervasive and global phenomenon. Many different countries employ significant numbers of people and resources to manage and manipulate public opinion online, sometimes targeting domestic audiences and sometimes targeting foreign publics,"[51] the researchers wrote.

The researchers found evidence of political manipulation via social media as far back as 2010. Seven years later, they had uncovered organized efforts in twenty-eight countries. Both authoritarian governments and democracies were involved in social media manipulation. In authoritarian countries, the government often coordinated and funded manipulation campaigns on social media. In democratic countries, political parties were more likely to be the main organizers of social media manipulation efforts.

> "Many different countries employ significant numbers of people and resources to manage and manipulate public opinion online, sometimes targeting domestic audiences and sometimes targeting foreign publics."[51]
>
> —A 2017 report from Oxford University's Computational Propaganda Research Project

Organized social media manipulation takes many forms. Cybertroops create official government websites and applications to spread content. They use social media accounts—either real, fake, or automated bots—to interact with social media users and spread false and misleading information to promote a political agenda. Sometimes these efforts target citizens in their own countries; other times they target the populations of other countries. They create and post content such as blog posts, pictures, and videos. Whereas some cybertroops focus on positive, progovernment messages when engaging with the public on social media, others use negative tactics, such as harassing, trolling, or threatening users who have dissenting opinions. "There is no doubt that individual social media users can spread hate speech, troll other users, or set up automated political communication campaigns. Unfortunately, this is also an organized phenomenon, with major governments and political parties dedicating significant resources towards the use of social media for public opinion manipulation,"[52] write researchers Samantha Bradshaw and Philip N. Howard, the authors of the 2017 Oxford University report.

An Important Role in Recent Elections

Before the 2016 presidential election, few Americans had heard of fake news. However, the fake news machine launched into overdrive during the months and weeks leading up to and after the election. Organized efforts to spread false information reached millions of people. Facebook estimates that 126 million of its users saw false articles and posts spread by Russian sources. Twitter has identified more than twenty-seven hundred accounts established by Russian groups that tweeted 1.4 million times in 2016 alone. And a Buzzfeed analysis found that the most widely shared fake news stories involved Trump and Clinton and generated millions of shares, reactions, and comments. According to the Buzzfeed analysis, the majority of these posts attempted to sway public opinion in favor of Trump or create a more negative image of Clinton. Still, it is unclear how much of a real-world effect fake news had on the election outcome, either by changing a person's vote from one candidate to the other or causing a person to not vote at all.

According to a 2017 report, democracy watchdog organization Freedom House found that fake news played an important role in recent elections in at least seventeen other countries. In Kenya, for example, false reports bearing CNN and BBC logos spread across Facebook and WhatsApp in the weeks before the country's presidential election. At first glance, the fake reports seemed real. One report used segments from an actual CNN broadcast but added a fake voiceover. The speaker falsely implied that a recent poll showed the incumbent leading his opponent by a wide margin. In truth, the margin between the two candidates was close, with neither having enough projected votes to win the

Ongoing Election Interference

Most intelligence and security experts believe that election interference will continue well into the future. In the United States, intelligence agencies were expecting Russia and other foreign governments to attempt to interfere in the 2018 midterm and state elections as well as future political contests. They predicted that Russian intelligence agencies and other potential manipulators would attempt to spread more false information through fake online accounts and social media. The goal of these agencies and individuals has been and will continue to be to destabilize US society by creating and magnifying political and social division. Director of National Intelligence Dan Coats says such interference is a serious problem. "Cyber has been a game-changer in many, many ways. The United States is under attack—now."

Quoted in Deb Reichmann, "U.S. Intelligence Agencies Expect Russia to Target 2018 Midterms," *PBS NewsHour*, February 13, 2018. www.pbs.org.

election outright. The fake poll was widely shared on social media. Alphonce Shiundu, the Kenya editor of Africa Check, a not-for-profit fact-checking organization that promotes accuracy in media, worries about the effect of bogus reports like these. "People who don't watch CNN or the BBC would not know that these videos were fake," Shiundu explains. "When this fake report is putting [incumbent president Uhuru] Kenyatta ahead, and you're sending this video to Kenyatta's stronghold, it just reinforces the belief that he has the numbers and he's going to win." Convincing fake news videos like this one might be able to sway undecided voters who also pass the fake news to family and friends. "If they send that video to a community group or a family group in the village—they will believe that it's true—and are likely to vote for the side that has the numbers,"[53] says Shiundu.

Manipulation with Personal Data

With billions of users worldwide, social media affords those who seek to alter and manipulate public opinion yet another opportunity. Social media companies collect massive amounts of personal information from their users. The data is sorted to identify users with certain characteristics, habits, or interests. Using this data, businesses can target consumers who are most likely to buy their products. This is basically how online advertising works.

Individuals or entities who want to manipulate public opinion on political issues can do something similar. If they can direct the right political message to the right group of people at the right time, they can influence attitudes and actions. And most of the time, users do not even realize that they are being targeted with manipulative messaging. All that is needed is the data. In 2014 a company called Cambridge Analytica (CA) figured out a way to get this type of information. CA was hired by the Trump campaign to assist with digital marketing, data analysis, and database creation. The company managed to gain access to private information on more than 50 million Facebook users. It used that information to identify the personalities of voters and target them with messages designed to influence their opinions and behavior.

An image of a father-son hunting trip might evoke strong positive feelings. Images like this were used in highly personalized political ads that were created—without user knowledge—from Facebook personality surveys and other sources.

CA researchers began by asking some thirty-two thousand Facebook users to take a detailed personality survey for a nominal payment. The survey required the users to log in with their Facebook account. The online survey collected the participants' responses, along with private information from their Facebook profiles. Importantly, it also collected data from their friends' accounts, ultimately gathering the profiles of more than 50 million users. The data included information about the users' identities, education, location, relationship status, employers, friend networks, and what they liked on social media. The company combined this data with other information from polls, voter records, and online activity to create a personality model for the users.

With the personality profiles, the company could target users with highly personalized political advertising. A pro–gun rights message, for example, can be made more effective if it appeals to individual interests or needs. Voters who have strong fears about personal safety are likely to respond to an ad that shows the hand of an intruder smashing a window because it appeals to their belief that guns are important for protection. Another voter, who places emphasis on traditions and family, might respond to a different pro–gun rights image, such as one that shows a man and his son or daughter enjoying the experience of hunting together. Molding a message to appeal to different personalities can help a candidate connect better with potential voters. Most of the people whose information was gathered by CA did not know it was being collected or believed it would be used for academic purposes, not for targeted political ads. People involved in the Trump campaign say they never used the data CA acquired from Facebook. Instead, CA focused more on online fund-raising, reaching undecided voters, and increasing voter turnout.

The increasing use of false information online to influence public opinion on political matters, candidates, and elections is a concerning trend. Fake news becomes even more dangerous when it has the potential to change people's minds about issues and influence how or whether they vote.

CHAPTER FIVE

Fighting Fake News and Other Manipulation Techniques

Around the world, there is a growing debate on how to fix the problem of fake news and other online public manipulation. Various solutions have surfaced. One solution places responsibility for policing online content on social media and technology companies. Another is for governments to regulate access to online platforms. A third solution pushes the idea that users need to educate themselves about the content they read and view online and learn how to identify false and manipulative news and information. Many experts argue that some combination of these and other ideas will be needed.

Acknowledging the Problem

Social media companies initially scoffed at claims that Russian agents had used their platforms to engage in a massive disinformation campaign aimed at manipulating US voter sentiments during the 2016 presidential election. But in late 2017 Facebook founder and chief executive officer Mark Zuckerberg publicly acknowledged that more than 126 million of its users may have been exposed to political ads and fake news purchased by the Russian-linked Internet Research Agency. In addition to Zuckerberg's admission, Google also acknowledged that Russian agents uploaded more than one thousand videos on its YouTube platform, and Twitter executives said that Russian agents published more than 131,000 messages on its platform.

Faced with the scope of manipulation on their sites, the tech giants are taking steps to stop fake news in its tracks. "The abuse of our platform to attempt state-sponsored manipulation of elections is a new challenge for us—and one that we are determined to meet,"[54] Twitter's acting general counsel, Sean Edgett, said during a 2017 hearing before Congress.

Facebook Acts

Each company is tackling the problem in its own way. Facebook has begun asking its users to flag questionable stories. When enough users flag the same story, the company sends it to an outside fact-checking organization. If the story fails fact-checking, Facebook publicly flags it as being disputed by a third-party fact-checker. Users can click on a link that explains why the story is disputed. If they share the story, they receive another warning about its questionable accuracy. In addition, Facebook is focusing on identifying fake news intended to influence an election. "We're ramping up our fact-checking efforts to fight false news around elections . . . expanding beyond links to photos and videos, and increasing transparency,"[55] says Facebook product manager Tessa Lyons.

> "We're ramping up our fact-checking efforts to fight false news around elections."[55]
>
> —Facebook product manager Tessa Lyons

Along with increased fact-checking, Facebook is working to remove fake accounts and pages. The social media giant announced that during the first three months of 2018, it had disabled 583 million fake accounts. The company has become more vigilant in its efforts to identify accounts and pages controlled by the Russian Internet Research Agency. US intelligence services have linked this group to fake news and divisive content on social media during the 2016 presidential election. In April 2018 Facebook announced that it had removed more than 270 accounts and pages controlled by this group. The Russian agency, Zuckerberg states, "has repeatedly acted to deceive people and manipulate people around the world, and we don't want them on Facebook anywhere."[56]

Facebook has also changed its review process for paid political advertising. The goal is to prevent foreign operatives from purchasing ads aimed at interfering in the American political process. Commenting on efforts being made by Facebook to prevent interference in the 2018 midterm elections, product management director Rob Leathern noted that "in the run up to the US midterm elections, advertisers will have to verify and confirm who they are and where they are located in the US."[57] Advertisers were being asked to submit government-issued identification and provide a physical mailing address. They were also required to respond to a mailed verification letter and to disclose the political party, candidate, organization, or business they represented.

Facebook founder and chief executive officer Mark Zuckerberg testifies at a Senate committee hearing in 2018. Zuckerberg has acknowledged that more than 126 million users may have been exposed to Russian-backed political ads and fake news.

ark Zuckerberg

Twitter and Google Take Steps

Twitter has also taken steps to identify and remove fake accounts and automated accounts. In 2018 Twitter reported that it was locking nearly 10 million suspicious accounts per week and removing more for violating the site's anti-spam rules. When an account is locked, it is blocked from posting or interacting with other Twitter users. The company also announced that it would be removing the tens of millions of blocked accounts from users' follower lists in an effort to restore trust in the social media platform. Many believe it is a step in the right direction. "People will believe more and read more on Twitter if they know there is less bot activity and more human activity," says Keith Weed, the chief marketing officer of the consumer goods corporation Unilever. "I would encourage and ask others to follow."[58]

Google, which owns YouTube, has also taken steps to combat fake news. Computer-savvy users have been able to manipulate Google's algorithm to get fake news sites placed higher

Identifying Manipulated Photos and Videos

Some types of fake news involve manipulated photos or videos. For example, after the 2018 school shooting in Parkland, Florida, a fake photo of survivor and gun control advocate Emma González ripping up the US Constitution spread across social media and sparked outrage from thousands of people. Most people had no way of knowing that the photo had been fabricated.

Now, researchers with the Defense Advanced Research Projects Agency (DARPA) are developing an automated tool to fight this type of online manipulation. Their work focuses on developing tools that can detect a manipulated photo, video, or audio file and provide detailed information about how the file was altered. Once the tools are complete, DARPA plans to work directly with tech companies to implement them on their platforms, allowing the companies to identify potentially fake content in seconds.

in search results. Paid advertising has also been affected. Fake news creators have paid for ads that link to their sites to appear in Google ads. On YouTube, fake news sites have posted false and misleading videos that were viewed and shared by millions of users. To combat fake news on its platforms, Google has refined its search engine algorithm to return authoritative sources higher in search results and questionable sites lower. The company has also partnered with fact-checking organizations to identify fake news that appears on both Google and YouTube. Advertising is also under scrutiny. Google is now requiring advertisers to identify themselves. It is also requiring buyers of political ads to disclose information about who paid for the ads.

In 2018 Google announced the launch of the Google News Initiative (GNI), a multifaceted initiative to improve journalism in the digital age. Since its launch, the GNI has provided funding to help news outlets create compelling online news and build sustainable video operations and has invested in product features on YouTube that allow it to prominently feature authoritative news sources. "On our own platforms, we're focused on combating misinformation during breaking news situations. Bad actors often target breaking news on Google platforms, increasing the likelihood that people are exposed to inaccurate content. So we've trained our systems to recognize these events and adjust our signals toward more authoritative content,"[59] writes Philipp Schindler, Google's chief business officer. The company has made similar changes on YouTube. As part of the GNI, Google is launching the Disinfo Lab to fight disinformation during election cycles and breaking news events. The company has also teamed up with the Poynter Institute and the Local Media Association to launch MediaWise, a project designed to educate young Americans in digital information literacy.

Yet many are skeptical that social media companies can effectively address fake news. Some believe that the platforms have done too little, too late. "I don't feel like it's working at all," says a journalist who does fact-checking for Facebook. "The fake information is still going viral and spreading rapidly."[60] Melissa Zimdars, an assistant professor of communication and media at Merrimack College agrees that Facebook's fact-checking system to combat fake news is falling short. "My initial read on it is it's ultimately kind of a PR move. It's cheap to do. It's easy. It doesn't actually require them to do anything."[61] Others point out that these companies make money through advertising and by generating more user engagement with content—regardless of whether that content is true or false. Critics say this revenue model gives them little incentive to shut down fake news, especially if it decreases their profits.

Artificial Intelligence

The sheer volume of fake news spreading across the Internet makes it impossible for human users to find, identify, and remove every fake story, picture, and video. Therefore, several tech companies are developing computer algorithms and artificial intelligence (AI) tools that can be used to identify suspicious stories. One such company, AdVerif.ai, began public testing of its new AI software in 2017. According to the company, the software can detect fake stories, nudity, malware, and other unwanted content. It does this by scanning content and searching for common signs that something is wrong, such as a headline that does not match body text or a headline with too many capital letters. (This is similar to how people can recognize phishing e-mails by the number of misspelled words and grammatical errors.) The software also cross-checks each story with a frequently updated database of thousands of fake and real stories. The company provides its clients with a report for each story the software has reviewed and assigns a score that assesses the likelihood that it is factual.

In testing, the AdVerif.ai program correctly classified articles from the Onion as satire. The software also identified a Twitter account that used a logo but promoted links that were not associated with the brand it was portraying. It correctly identified a fake news story that appeared on several sites. Still, the software was not perfect. Some stories that later proved to be false were not flagged. For example, a post about an NFL player supposedly burning the American flag in his team's locker room was not flagged as fake even through it was proved to be false. To help the software learn and improve as it works, the company manually updates its list of fake stories.

Social media companies like Facebook are also turning to AI to fight fake news. In July 2018 Facebook announced that it was acquiring the London-based start-up Bloomsbury AI. Currently, human workers oversee Facebook's content. They inspect flagged and reported posts and decide whether content violates the network's rules or whether it is fake news, hate speech, or other offensive material. Facebook plans to increase its AI capabilities so that algorithms perform more of this work, improving productivity and allowing the platform to review more content, faster. Eventually, the company hopes to develop AI that can understand text, images, and video well enough to effectively review content on the platform. Bloomsbury AI's team specializes in programming computers to process and analyze large amounts of language data, like that found on Facebook posts. On the Facebook Academics page, the company posted, "The Bloomsbury team has built a leading expertise in machine reading and understanding unstructured documents in natural language in order to answer any question. Their expertise will strengthen Facebook's efforts in natural language processing research, and help us further understand natural language and its applications."[62]

Government Efforts

While social media and technology companies are working to prevent and remove fake news from their platforms, governments around the world are also taking action. Many countries are considering or adopting new laws and regulations. A law passed in France in 2018 gives French authorities the power to determine

Balancing Free Expression and Restrictions on Fake News

Most Americans do not want the government to limit free expression, but they would support action by technology companies to restrict false information. This is the finding of a 2018 Pew Research Center survey. When asked whether the US government should restrict false information online even if it limits free expression, 58 percent (nearly six in ten Americans) said freedom of information should be protected even if it means the presence of fake news online. On the other hand, when asked whether tech companies should take steps to restrict false information even if it limits free expression, 56 percent said they would support those restrictions.

The trade-off between more government restrictions on free expression and less false information online lacks support from nearly all demographic groups, but this position is strongest among younger Americans. "At least six-in-ten adults ages 18 to 29 (65%) and 30 to 49 (62%) prefer no government restrictions on information flow compared with 53% of those 50 to 64 and 48% of those 65 and older," the Pew report states. People in the younger age groups are also less supportive than older Americans of restrictions being imposed by tech companies.

Quoted in Amy Mitchell et al., "Americans Favor Protecting Information Freedoms over Government Steps to Restrict False News Online," Pew Research Center, April 19, 2018. www.journalism.org.

whether content is manipulative and, if so, remove it from social media. The law also enables authorities to block sites that publish fake and manipulative content. Political candidates can also sue for the removal of contested news reports during an election period. The law will also require social media platforms such as Facebook and Twitter to publish who purchased sponsored content or campaign ads and how much they paid. "I am delighted by Parliament's passing of a balanced and effective text that rises to the magnitude of the issue, a text that will be a precious tool for better protecting our democracy,"[63] says Culture Minister Françoise Nyssen.

The German parliament has also taken action. In 2017 it adopted a law that bans the posting of false information and hate speech on social media. Under the law, social media platforms like Facebook and Twitter can face fines of up to 50 million euros if they fail to take down false content or hate speech on their sites within twenty-four hours of being notified about it. Other European countries, including Sweden, Ireland, and the Czech Republic, are also considering legislation to combat fake news.

The issue of foreign influence on elections, not just through fake websites and stories but also through online political advertisements, has also gained the attention of US lawmakers. A bill being considered by Congress would require online political ads to follow rules similar to those for political ads in newspapers and on television. If passed, companies like Google and Facebook would be required to maintain copies of political ads before they disappear from the Internet and make them publicly available to review and compare against other political ads. The companies would also be required to disclose information on the types of users targeted by the ads, the ad buyers, and the rates charged for the ads.

Critics of laws like these warn that increased government regulation can restrict free speech. Laws that require social media companies to decide which content to delete may cross the line into censorship and threaten freedom of expression. Similarly, legislation aimed at restricting fake news may also give the government too much control over what information remains online for citizens to consume. Yin Yin Lu, a researcher at the Oxford Internet Institute, believes that the responsibility for dealing with fake news should lie with social media platforms and users rather than government. "It should be the responsibility of the platforms to implement a design solution that would indicate visually the quality of news sources that were shared. This would allow users themselves to determine whether or not they should trust them,"[64] she says.

> "It should be the responsibility of the platforms to implement a design solution that would indicate visually the quality of news sources that were shared. This would allow users themselves to determine whether or not they should trust them."[64]
>
> —Yin Yin Lu, a researcher at the Oxford Internet Institute

Education Efforts

Teaching people how to evaluate the content they encounter online might be one of the most effective ways to limit the spread of fake news. News literacy programs teach people how to evaluate news sources and not accept what they read and see simply at face value. These literacy programs also teach users to expand their sources of information and follow a variety of people, representing different viewpoints. Howard Schneider, the dean of the School of Journalism at Stony Brook University, believes that teaching readers how to evaluate news and sources is critical to stopping the spread of fake news in the digital age. Schneider contends that

> new technologies have brought wondrous benefits but also made it easier for malevolent actors motivated by ideology or profit to create and virally spread authentic-looking reports and images. . . . The deficits in the public's ability . . . to critically identify and evaluate reliable news and information, are widespread . . . and go way beyond the issue of our current preoccupation with patently fake or fabricated news. They not only continue to undermine trust in the news media but in our democratic institutions.[65]

In Italy, a news education program was tested in eight thousand high schools in 2017. The goal of the program is to train students who live in a social media world how to recognize fake news and conspiracy theories. "Fake news drips drops of poison into our daily web diet and we end up infected without even realizing it," says Laura Boldrini, the president of the lower house of the Italian parliament, who has spearheaded the project with the Italian Ministry of Education.

> "Fake news drips drops of poison into our daily web diet and we end up infected without even realizing it. It's only right to give these kids the possibility to defend themselves from lies."[66]
>
> —Laura Boldrini, the president of the lower house of the Italian parliament

A Connecticut teacher librarian works with a high school freshman during a media literacy skills class. Various efforts are under way in countries around the world to teach students how to be informed news consumers.

"It's only right to give these kids the possibility to defend themselves from lies,"[66] she adds.

In the United States, the News Literacy Project (NLP) is one example of efforts to teach students how to decide what is real in the digital age. A national nonprofit organization, the NLP provides middle school and high school students with skills they need to become smart and informed news consumers. Through classroom and online lessons, the program aims to teach students that all information is not equal. The program also encourages students to produce and share information that is accurate and fair.

Working Together for the Truth

In the United States and around the world, efforts to combat fake news and the manipulation of public opinion online are being undertaken by social media platforms, technology companies, governments, educators, and individual users. Being aware of fake news and the ways in which it spreads is the first step toward stopping it. "It's such a complex problem that it must be attacked from every angle,"[67] says computer scientist Filippo Menczer.

SOURCE NOTES

Introduction: Manipulating Public Opinion

1. Quoted in M. Mitchell Waldrop, "News Feature: The Genuine Problem of Fake News," *Proceedings of the National Academy of Sciences of the United States of America*, vol. 114, no. 48, November 28, 2017. www.pnas.org.
2. Quoted in Waldrop, "News Feature."
3. Quoted in Aaron Blake, "A New Study Suggests Fake News Might Have Won Donald Trump the 2016 Election," *Washington Post*, April 3, 2018. www.washingtonpost.com.
4. Quoted in David Cox, "Fake News Is Still a Problem. Is AI the Solution?," NBC News, February 15, 2018. www.nbcnews.com.
5. Quoted in Monmouth University Polling Institute, "'Fake News' Threat to Media; Editorial Decisions, Outside Actors at Fault," April 2, 2018. www.monmouth.edu.
6. Quoted in Indiana University–Bloomington, "Large-Scale Scientific Investigation Needed to Combat Fake News, IU Researcher Says," March 8, 2018. https://news.iu.edu.

Chapter One: The New Look of Fake News

7. Quoted in Jackie Mansky, "The Age Old Problem of 'Fake News,'" *Smithsonian Magazine*, May 7, 2018. www.smithsonianmag.com.
8. Quoted in Mansky, "The Age Old Problem of 'Fake News.'"
9. Quoted in Mansky, "The Age Old Problem of 'Fake News.'"
10. Quoted in Mansky, "The Age Old Problem of 'Fake News.'"
11. Quoted in Mathew Ingram, "Fake News Is Part of a Bigger Problem: Automated Propaganda," *Columbia Journalism Review,* February 22, 2018. www.cjr.org.
12. Quoted in Emma Jane Kirby, "The City Getting Rich from Fake News," BBC News, December 5, 2016. www.bbcnews.com.
13. Quoted in Kirby, "The City Getting Rich from Fake News."
14. Quoted in Erik Hedegaard, "How a Fake Newsman Accidentally Helped Trump Win the White House," *Rolling Stone*, November 29, 2016. www.rollingstone.com.

15. Quoted in Tess Townsend, "The Bizarre Truth Behind the Biggest Pro-Trump Facebook Hoaxes," Inc.com. www.inc.com.

16. Quoted in Dianne de Guzman, "Report: Fake Election News Outperformed Real News on Facebook Ahead of the Election," *San Francisco Chronicle*, November 16, 2016. www.sfchronicle.com.

17. Zoe Hawkins, "Securing Democracy in the Digital Age," Australian Strategic Policy Institute, May 29, 2017. https://s3-ap-southeast-2.amazonaws.com/ad-aspi/2017-08/ASPI%20Securing%20Democracy.pdf.

18. Zoe Hawkins, "Securing Democracy in the Digital Age."

19. Sinan Aral, "Truth, Disrupted," *Harvard Business Review*, July 17, 2018. https://hbr.org.

20. Quoted in Kenneth Rapoza, "Can 'Fake News' Impact the Stock Market?," *Forbes*, February 26, 2017. www.forbes.com.

21. Quoted in Hannah Kuchler, "Companies Scramble to Combat 'Fake News,'" *Financial Times,* August 22, 2017. www.ft.com.

Chapter Two: Why Is Fake News So Hard to Spot?

22. Quoted in Laurie Kellman and Jonathan Drew, "Fact or Fiction? Trump's False Claims, Attacks on 'Fake News' Leave Americans Confused," Global News, January 14, 2018. https://globalnews.ca.

23. Quoted in Kellman and Drew, "Fact or Fiction?"

24. Quoted in Kellman and Drew, "Fact or Fiction?"

25. Quoted in Stephanie Thurrott, "How to Spot Fake News in Your Social Media Feed," NBC News, March 13, 2018. www.nbcnews.com.

26. Quoted in Christopher Rosen, "All the Times Donald Trump Has Called the Media 'Fake News' on Twitter," *Entertainment Weekly*, July 24, 2017. https://ew.com.

27. Quoted in Editorial Board, "A Free Press Needs You," *New York Times,* August 15, 2018. www.nytimes.com.

28. Quoted in Rick Gladstone, "Syria's Assad Sends Signals to Trump in Interview," *New York Times,* February 10, 2017. www.nytimes.com.

29. Quoted in Mike Wendling, "The (Almost) Complete History of Fake News," *BBC Trending* (blog), BBC News, January 22, 2018. www.bbcnews.com.

30. Quoted in Wendling, "The (Almost) Complete History of Fake News."

31. Onion, "Cash-Strapped Zuckerberg Forced To Sell 11 Million Facebook Users," September 17, 2018. www.theonion.com.

32. Quoted in Joshua Gillin, "Fake News Story Twists Paul Ryan's Words on Poor People's Health Care Coverage," Politifact .com, July 11, 2017. www.politifact.com.

33. Quoted in Valerie Boey, "School Official Says He Was Duped by 'Fake News' When Claiming Student Was 'Crisis Actor,'" Fox10Phoenix.com, February 21, 2018. www.fox10phoenix .com.

34. Quoted in Ohio State University "Reliance on 'Gut Feelings' Linked to Belief in Fake News, Study Finds," September 18, 2017. https://news.osu.edu.

35. Quoted in Vignesh Ramachandran, "How Do You Identify Fake News?," ProPublica Illinois, April 4, 2018. www.pro publica.org.

Chapter Three: Social Media's Role in the Spread of Fake News

36. Samantha Bradshaw and Philip N. Howard, "Why Does Junk News Spread So Quickly Across Social Media? Algorithms, Advertising and Exposure in Public Life," Knight Foundation, January 29, 2018. https://kf-site-production.s3.amazonaws .com/media_elements/files/000/000/142/original/Topos_KF _White-Paper_Howard_V1_ado.pdf.

37. Donald J. Trump (@realdonaldtrump), "I have stated my concerns with Amazon . . . ," Twitter, March 29, 2018, 4:57 a.m. https://twitter.com.

38. Quoted in Maggie Fox, "Fake News: Lies Spread Faster on Social Media than Truth Does," NBC News, March 8, 2018. www.nbcnews.com.

39. Quoted in Fox, "Fake News."

40. Quoted in Fox, "Fake News."

41. Quoted in Sapna Maheshwari, "How Fake News Goes Viral: A Case Study," *New York Times,* November 20, 2016. www .nytimes.com.

42. Quoted in Maheshwari, "How Fake News Goes Viral."
43. Quoted in Cory Nealon, "During Disasters, Active Twitter Users Likely to Spread Falsehoods," University at Buffalo, May 11, 2018. www.buffalo.edu.
44. Bradshaw and Howard, "Why Does Junk News Spread So Quickly Across Social Media?"
45. Quoted in Alfred Ng, "How Russian Trolls Lie Their Way to the Top of Your News Feed," CNET, October 30, 2017. www.cnet.com.

Chapter Four: Election Interference

46. Quoted in Matt Apuzzo and Sharon LaFraniere, "13 Russians Indicted as Mueller Reveals Effort to Aid Trump Campaign," *New York Times,* February 16, 2018. www.nytimes.com.
47. Quoted in Apuzzo and LaFraniere, "13 Russians Indicted as Mueller Reveals Effort to Aid Trump Campaign."
48. Quoted in Kathryn Watson, "Russian Intelligence Officers Indicted in DNC Hacking," CBS News, July 13, 2018. www.cbsnews.com.
49. Quoted in Craig Timberg, "Spreading Fake News Becomes Standard Practice for Governments Across the World," *Washington Post*, July 17, 2017. www.washingtonpost.com.
50. Quoted in Kim Willsher and Jon Henley, "Emmanuel Macron's Campaign Hacked on Eve of French Election," *Guardian* (Manchester, UK), May 6, 2017. www.theguardian.com.
51. Samantha Bradshaw and Philip N. Howard, "Troops, Trolls and Troublemakers: A Global Inventory of Organized Social Media Manipulation," Working Paper 2017.12, Computational Propaganda Research Project. http://comprop.oii.ox.ac.uk.
52. Bradshaw and Howard, "Troops, Trolls and Troublemakers."
53. Quoted in Farai Sevenzo, "Kenya Election: Fake CNN, BBC Reports Target Voters," CNN, August 1, 2017. https://edition.cnn.com.

Chapter Five: Fighting Fake News and Other Manipulation Techniques

54. Quoted in Cecilia Kang, Nicholas Fandos, and Mike Isaac, "Tech Executives Are Contrite About Election Meddling, but Make Few Promises on Capitol Hill," *New York Times,* October 31, 2017. www.nytimes.com.

55. Quoted in Rob LeFebvre, "Facebook Is Stepping Up Its Fight Against Fake News," Engadget, March 29, 2018. www.engadget.com.
56. Quoted in Scott Shane, "Facebook Removes More Accounts Tied to Russian 'Troll Factory,'" *New York Times,* April 3, 2018. www.nytimes.com.
57. Quoted in LeFebvre, "Facebook Is Stepping Up Its Fight Against Fake News."
58. Quoted in Nicholas Confessore and Gabriel J.X. Dance, "Battling Fake Accounts, Twitter to Slash Millions of Followers," *New York Times,* July 11, 2018. www.nytimes.com.
59. Philipp Schindler, "The Google News Initiative: Building a Stronger Future for News," *Google News Initiative* (blog), Google, March 20, 2018. www.blog.google.
60. Quoted in Sam Levin, "'Way Too Little, Way Too Late': Facebook's Factcheckers Say Effort Is Failing," *Guardian* (Manchester, UK), November 13, 2017. www.theguardian.com.
61. Sam Levin, "Facebook Promised to Tackle Fake News. But the Evidence Shows It's Not Working," *Guardian* (Manchester, UK), May 16, 2017. www.theguardian.com.
62. Facebook Academics, "We're excited to announce that the team behind Bloomsbury AI has agreed to join Facebook in London," Facebook, July 3, 2018. www.facebook.com.
63. Quoted in Zachary Young, "French Parliament Passes Law Against 'Fake News,'" Politico, July 4, 2018. www.politico.eu.
64. Quoted in Richard Friday, "Fake News Laws Are Threatening Free Speech on a Global Scale," *Wired,* April 5, 2018. www.wired.co.uk.
65. Howard Schneider, "How News Literacy Programs Can Help Journalists Earn Back Trust," *Quill,* March 12, 2018. https://quill.spjnetwork.org.
66. Quoted in Jason Horowitz, "In Italian Schools, Reading, Writing and Recognizing Fake News," *New York Times*, October 18, 2017. www.nytimes.com.
67. Quoted in Dom Galeon, "Massive Study of Fake News May Reveal Why It Spreads So Easily," Futurism, March 8, 2018. https://futurism.com.

SIX WAYS TO EVALUATE INFORMATION

NewseumED, part of the education outreach group of the Newseum in Washington, DC, has created a tool to help young readers evaluate information. The six ways to evaluate information spell the word *ESCAPE*—which forms the title, "ESCAPE Junk News." The Newseum is an interactive museum whose mission is to increase public understanding of the importance of a free press and the First Amendment.

E **Is for Evidence: Do the Facts Hold Up?**
Look for information you can verify.
Names • Numbers • Places • Documents

S **Is for Source: Who Made This and Can I Trust Them?**
Trace who has touched the story.
Authors • Publishers • Funders • Aggregators • Social media users

C **Is for Context: What Is the Big Picture?**
Consider if this is the whole story and weigh other forces surrounding it.
Current events • Cultural trends • Political goals • Financial pressures

A **Is for Audience: Who Is the Intended Audience?**
Look for attempts to appeal to specific groups or types of people.
Image choices • Presentation techniques • Language • Content

P **Is for Purpose: Why Was This Made?**
Look for clues to the motivation.
The publisher's mission • Persuasive language or images • Moneymaking tactics • Stated or unstated agendas • Calls to action

E **Is for Execution: How Is This Information Presented?**
Consider how the way it is made affects the impact.
Style • Grammar • Tone • Image choices • Placement and layout

NewseumED, "Download an 'E.S.C.A.P.E. Junk News Poster, Bookmark." https://newseumed.org/escape.

ORGANIZATIONS TO CONTACT

AP Fact Check
www.apnews.com/tag/APFactCheck

This website is the fact-checking hub of the Associated Press news agency. It monitors and explains the veracity of public statements made by political figures.

Center for Media Literacy
22603 Pacific Coast Hwy., #549
Malibu, CA 90265
www.medialit.org

The Center for Media Literacy is an educational organization that provides media literacy education to help citizens learn to develop the skills needed to analyze, evaluate, create, and participate in today's media.

Center for News Literacy
www.centerfornewsliteracy.org

Located at Stony Brook University, the Center for News Literacy creates programs to educate college and high school students and the general public about news literacy.

FactCheck.org
www.factcheck.org

This website is affiliated with the Annenberg Foundation at the University of Pennsylvania. It evaluates the truth of statements made by public figures, especially politicians.

Media Bias/Fact Check
https://mediabiasfactcheck.com

This website lists various media sources and their political leanings, sorted into categories such as conspiracy, satire, fake news, and more.

News Literacy Project

5335 Wisconsin Ave. NW, Suite 440
Washington, DC 20015
https://newslit.org

The News Literacy Project is a national education nonprofit offering nonpartisan, independent programs that teach students how to know what to believe in the digital age.

PolitiFact

www.politifact.com

This website focuses on fact-checking, especially statements made by political figures and political interest groups.

Snopes

www.snopes.com

Snopes is an independent website that was originally devoted to urban legends. It has since expanded to cover fact-checking of statements about the world of politics, entertainment, and culture.

FOR FURTHER RESEARCH

Books

Sharyl Attkisson, *The Smear: How Shady Political Operatives and Fake News Control What You See, What You Think, and How You Vote*. New York: HarperCollins, 2017.

Donald A. Barclay, *Fake News, Propaganda, and Plain Old Lies: How to Find Trustworthy Information in the Digital Age*. Lanham, MD: Rowman & Littlefield, 2018.

Bruce Bartlett, *The Truth Matters: A Citizen's Guide to Separating Facts from Lies and Stopping Fake News in Its Tracks*. New York: Ten Speed, 2017.

Stephen Currie, *Sharing Posts: The Spread of Fake News*. San Diego: ReferencePoint, 2018.

Daniel J. Levitin, *Weaponized Lies: How to Think Critically in the Post-truth Era*. New York: Dutton, 2017.

Lee McIntyre, *Post-Truth*. Cambridge, MA: MIT Press, 2018.

Internet Sources

Samantha Bradshaw and Philip N. Howard, "Troops, Trolls and Troublemakers: A Global Inventory of Organized Social Media Manipulation," Working Paper 2017.12, Computational Research Propaganda Project. http://comprop.oii.ox.ac.uk/wp-content/up loads/sites/89/2017/07/Troops-Trolls-and-Troublemakers.pdf.

Samantha Bradshaw and Philip N. Howard, "Why Does Junk News Spread So Quickly Across Social Media? Algorithms, Advertising and Exposure in Public Life," Knight Foundation, January 29, 2018. https://kf-site-production.s3.amazonaws.com /media_elements/files/000/000/142/original/Topos_KF_White -Paper_Howard_V1_ado.pdf.

David Cox, "Fake News Is Still a Problem. Is AI the Solution?," NBC News, February 15, 2018. www.nbcnews.com/mach/sci ence/fake-news-still-problem-ai-solution-ncna848276.

Zoe Hawkins, "Securing Democracy in the Digital Age," Australian Strategic Policy Institute, May 29, 2017. https://s3-ap
-southeast-2.amazonaws.com/ad-aspi/2017-08/ASPI%20
Securing%20Democracy.pdf.

Alex Hern, "Cambridge Analytica: How Did It Turn Clicks into Votes?," *Guardian* (Manchester, UK), May 6, 2018. www.the
guardian.com/news/2018/may/06/cambridge-analytica-how
-turn-clicks-into-votes-christopher-wylie.

Jackie Mansky, "The Age Old Problem of 'Fake News,'" *Smithsonian Magazine*, May 7, 2018. www.smithsonianmag.com/history
/age-old-problem-fake-news-180968945.

Craig Timberg, "Spreading Fake News Becomes Standard Practice for Governments Across the World," *Washington Post*, July 17, 2017. www.washingtonpost.com/news
/the-switch/wp/2017/07/17/spreading-fake-news-becomes
-standard-practice-for-governments-across-the-world.

Mike Wendling, "The (Almost) Complete History of Fake News," *BBC Trending* (blog), BBC News, January 22, 2018. www.bbc
.com/news/blogs-trending-42724320.

INDEX

PICTURE CREDITS

ABOUT THE AUTHOR

Carla Mooney is the author of many books for young adults and children. She lives in Pittsburgh, Pennsylvania, with her husband and three children.